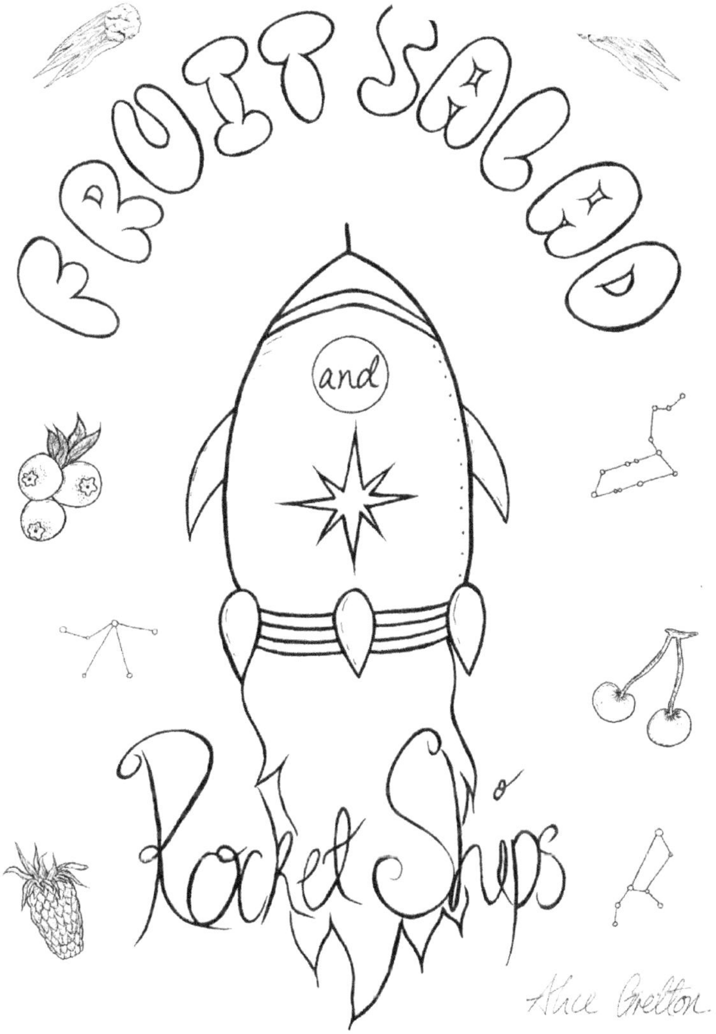
FRUIT SALAD
and
Rocket Ships

Copyright © 2024 Alice Gretton
Illustrations Copyright 2024 Alice Gretton

All rights reserved. This book or any portion thereof may not be reproduced or used in any manner whatsoever without the express written permission of the publisher except for the use of brief quotations in a book review or scholarly journal.

Published by Llais Newydd Poetry Press
Pontypridd
Wales

Proof edited by Dee Dickens

ISBN 9798377320180

For my inner child; I will always be proud of you.

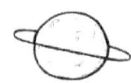

'It is here we find ourselves at the doormat to a stranger, soon to be a friend.'

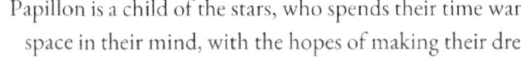

Papillon is a child of the stars, who spends their time wandering out to space in their mind, with the hopes of making their dream a reality.

Join the journey of Papillon as they adventure through space in their cardboard rocket ship, fuelled by fruit, to find the star they have named Hope.

"Alice's voice echoes from stage to page, effortlessly. Every smile, every wave of the hand, every unifying glance is present in each jot of ink. Her hallmark kindness, that makes her sets, events, and being such a pleasure to witness, shines through at all times. Even in the dark-spots, and isn't that what we all need?" - Sven Stears

"Drenched in originality, the antidote to apathy, allow Alice to show you beauty in the madness of being alive. This is a storybook for a traumatised inner child who is learning to heal. With a carefully guided redirection into the magic of a journey rather than lingering on the painful edges, each deftly original image in the collection builds the sense of being in a series of moving paintings with the brushstrokes of surrealism. Reality may be closing in around you, but this collection invites you to dance around your living room, around your planet, or amid the stars themselves. It's easy to be enchanted by this collection, Gretton has a beautiful control of juxtaposition. Within this collection you will find the aching beauty of finding happiness in a sad place, the childlike wonder of escapism immersed in the reality of a sharp world, and unrelenting love persevering in gorgeous original detail." - Kathryn O'Driscoll

"Alice Gretton is more than just a writer, she's a storyteller, a weaver of wondrous and magic words. Get ready to fall under her spell and never want to leave." - Dee Dickens

"Alice writes with the same immaculate control over words put on display if you've ever been fortunate enough to see a live performance for yourself. The way Fruit Salad and Rocket Ships can break your heart, sit in the dark with you before putting it back together and make you believe in love again (sometimes all three in the space of one poem) is what makes this collection a timeless classic. No one will teach you self-love quite like Alice and Papillon do on this journey to a star named Hope. They'll hold your hand every step of the way through the adventure and will have you convinced the cosmos is yours for the taking by the time you're home again. Their story is truly out of this world." - Joe Thomas

Thank you.

Hello, lovely reader.

I just wanted to take a minute to say, thank you so much for reading Fruit Salad and Rocket Ships. This book has been almost six years in the making, and I couldn't have done it without the loving support of my friends, family, fellow poets, and now you. I have poured my heart into this book, filling it with poems written on tear stained windowsills, bedroom floors and bathroom toilet seats. This book is who I am, and for you to take the time to read and appreciate my artwork, means the absolute world and beyond to me.

So, hello! It's lovely to meet you.

Now, because this book is completely raw, and there are many triggers and difficult subjects. I hope you have never had to relate to them, but if you have and need support, please reach out. Tell friends, family members, anyone you feel comfortable speaking to, and get it off your chest. Poetry and art is also an incredible outlet for emotion, so maybe it's time to pick up a pen.

Be kind to yourself. You are so important to this world, and I hope you know it.

All my love,

Table of Contents

TAKE OFF 4

CHAPTER ONE: Mirror house on the rainbow meteor..10

    The Oxford Dictionary 13

    Orchestra 16

    Home is not a choice 19

    Sunflowers on skirting boards 22

    Fridge magnets 24

    Bluebird 27

    Dying of the light from electric fish tanks 29

    I've grown accustomed to the idea of silence on my tv screen 31

CHAPTER TWO: Love letters Left in Orbit ..34

    Paris in the stars 36

    The Rainbow Archive 38

    Valentine with wool for eyes 43

    When you arrive 48

    The coping strategy 50

    Please don't make me your next supernova 53

    Jazmine 55

CHAPTER THREE: Hope is a black hole.......58

    This is the story of Daniel the space man 60

    Sorry, what did you say? 63

    I'm just a floating meteorite 66

Office mornings 67
The face of war (to rent) 69
The testimony of a stage-hand 71
The hurricane 73

CHAPTER FOUR: Home drive 78

Not to scale 80
I'm still in love with you 82
T-shirt 84
Saturn 86
A conversation with suicide 90

A ROCKY LANDING 94

BONUS CHAPTER: THE POLKA-DOT SHOP (and other absurdities) 96

The Polka Dot Shop 97
Bubbles 100
My period is a traffic light 103
You have a story in your skull 106

The story behind the salad 108

FRUIT SALAD AND ROCKET SHIPS

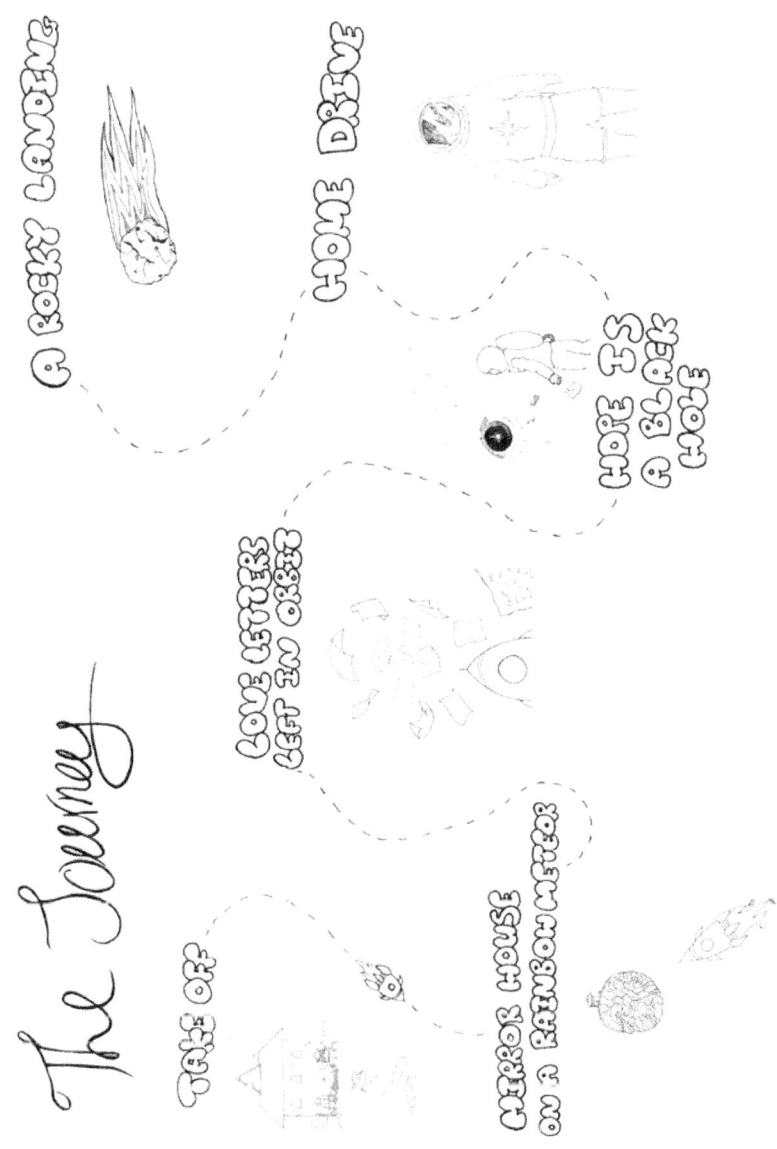

FRUIT SALAD AND ROCKET SHIPS

TAKE OFF

Time: 20:00
Location: 51°07'34"N 1°18'03"E
Feeling: Silent

It is here we find ourselves at the doormat to a stranger, soon to be a friend. There is night time blue painted onto the walls of this tinfoil house. The house tries not to yawn, so to not knock itself to the ground it is so desperately trying to stand upon. This is not a home of many colours, plenty of money, any worth. This house is weak at the knees held up by the needs of those who live inside of it.

Upon entering, shadows seep into the corners of the room. Blue paints itself into the skirting boards. The corridor ahead squeezes you as you pass through, nearly breathless when it spits you out into the room called living. Here sits a silent girl playing with dust rabbits, hopping across the fireplace, sitting dimly lit with warmth. The fire chuckles to keep her company. The girl smiles faintly at its auburn courage.

Two steps forward and a sharp left, you stumble upon a kitchen and an argument. Two eyebrows shout at two sharp lips that raise themselves into smiles when needed at dinner parties. They love each other, the faces that take the night. But it's hard to see in between the singing of anger that rattles the plates on the dinner table.

Three turns to the right, five steps and a look upwards, you find a staircase seemingly untrodden, leading to a small wooden door painted purple. This, dear reader, is where they sit. Hands folded in their lap, two wide eyes and a dainty button nose that twitches when they sniffle. This is Papillon. They sit, cross legged and stern, staring with a yearn at a window that daren't be open. In front of their feet, Papillon is reading of space and the wonders it entails. They have circled a star, named it hope, and have put their shoes on for running.

Here is the plan. They say, rubbing their hands in a shake.
Before they wake, I will be gone. I've carved the cardboard shape, I have got my space suit on. In a rocket ship built from my tin foil home, I will leave. And they will never know.

Papillon counts the clock like letters spelling out an exit sign. At five minutes to eleven, Papillon hears the rumbling of snores beneath the floorboards.
It is time. Papillon pauses. *I will leave tonight.*

Papillon fills their rocket to the brim with fruit and vegetables.
My nana says an apple a day keeps a doctor away, perhaps it shall keep my family at bay, perhaps this can be my fuel for the journey.
With naive wisdom and blind clarity, a sea of apples, oranges and greens fill their cardboard spaceship.
Papillon climbs inside.
There is silence in the room.

Nothing.

Papillon waits for what feels like lifetimes stacked upon each other,
timelines growing longer than the shadows on their window sill.

Nothing.

Papillon looks to the sky and mutters something of a wish.

Nothing.

Papillon stares with a cry at the stars who stare back at them. They sigh with a thousand lightyears of sorry.

Nothing.

Papillon bursts into a scream. The walls are folding in on them like origami caving in the air. Papillon despairs into a weep, that becomes a sleep, within seconds.

Then. In what seemed and felt like moments.

Rumble.

Crack.

Shake.

Papillon wakes to the grumbling belly of their rocket ship leaving the ground it had been resting on.

Could it be?

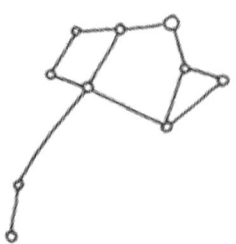

They could not believe the ground was telling the truth.

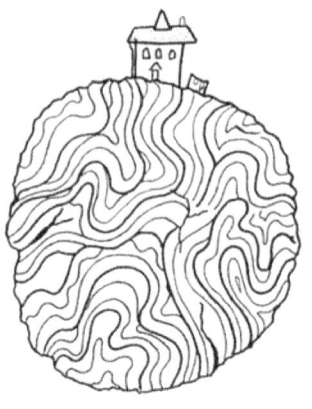

CHAPTER ONE: Mirror house on the rainbow meteor

Time: 22:00
Location: RA 17h 37m 39s | Dec -20° 10' 20"
Feeling: Breathless

With the catching of a breath, Papillon watches the colours of the changing world around them peel away. Fading greens, to darkened blues, to blackness, much alike the changing of a paint brush. They had done it. Flown away from the fear of sorry, the anger of silence, the overwhelming underwhelm of being happy in sadness. They were a whole masterpiece from home, and ahead of them? A blank canvas. Dark, speckled with stars like freckles, Papillon's eyes start to catch up with them. Connecting the stars like dot to dots, Papillon navigates their cardboard ship towards the ever so far yet never closer hope star, dancing at the heart of Aquarius. This was it. With a second caught breath, Papillon presses their paper pedal and propels towards the day they had yet to unpeel.

On route to this new day, Papillon spots what seemed to be a meteor dressed in technicolour. It

FRUIT SALAD AND ROCKET SHIPS

was rough around the edges, seemed scuffed and spun and scrambled, yet across its surface glistened blues, purples, yellows, all enunciated by the nearby sun. Filled with intrigue, Papillon decides on a pit stop on the colourful conundrum. An unanswered question never did seem to sit right with them.

With a grumble of the paper rocket's belly, Papillon landed with a clunk into a small blue crater. Step. This was a land their feet had never known yet felt walked upon before, from crater to core, unknowingly familiar. Step.

I feel as though I have been here once before.

Papillon began walking across the meteor's terrain. The sun's starlight settled on technicolour rock as far as the eye could see. Papillon's eyes moulded into kaleidoscopes of wonder and a heart so full it could burst and bleed the colours it could see for miles around. On their travels, Papillon passed unsteady rock bleeding colour, potholes of red, blue and green, hills of yellow and violet under their climbing feet. This was a place of warmth. This was a place of pain.

After climbing what seemed like a hundredth hill, Papillon came at the top. Jaws dropped. Eyes trying to stay in their sockets, hearts nearing a stop.

There is no way I could explain to you what mesmerising is. You would need to breathe it for yourself.

There was something shadowing the sun in the distance. A house, no larger than their tinfoil home, in fact identical in shape and its tired eyes for windows. This house was standing patiently in the epicentre of all colours combined. But the striking difference in this house to home; this house was made of mirrors.

Overflowing with fascination, Papillon chose to run. Papillon splashes through technicolour puddles, grazes their knee on a green rock, catches their breath on pink air. Each step splashes colour on their spacesuit, soaking their body head to toe in rainbow shades that Papillon remains unphased to in the journey.

This, once again, felt familiar. Felt comfortable. Felt real.

As they arrived at the house, Papillon realised there was no door. No staircase, bedroom, angry eyebrows or sunken fireplaces.

Only stood there. Coated in rainbow. Staring back, both silent, and smiling.

The Oxford Dictionary

The Oxford dictionary states that home is
the place where one lives permanently.
Well Oxford, I have never had a home.
You see permanence became pertinence
and personality clashes between
tea cups and cutlery.

She wanted to talk.
He wanted a fork.
She wanted fidelity
He wanted a fork
She wanted a clear road
and rode dreams of matrimony
He wanted a fork.

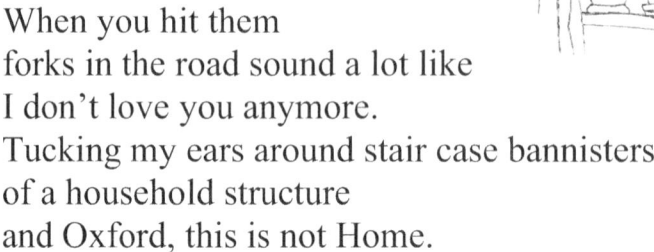

When you hit them
forks in the road sound a lot like
I don't love you anymore.
Tucking my ears around stair case bannisters
of a household structure
and Oxford, this is not Home.

Oxford dictionary fails to understand
the fragility of jelly houses.
And jelly babies live on trampolines
not knowing whether Home's been
on Aunt Lacey's sofa
or behind green grass doorways.

Jelly babies eat themselves away in cupboards.
They live a shelf life.
Presented to the visitors behind glass and fake smiles

the jelly baby exasperates every kind word
and white lies they can stick to sweet metaphors.
She's so sweet, they nod with closed eyes to each other,

and eat up each inch of jelly baby bullshit
that they can reach down from the cupboard.

Home is where the heart is well
my heart has never beat faster
than when running from everything that is home,
to you.

Oxford.
Take a pen and paper.
And sit on a seat you consider comfortable.

Write how comfort is Home.
Write how Home is the people that give home
made handmade brownies in brown wicca baskets

Write how Home is warm eyes in dim lit double beds
and soft lips while cooking pasta.
How every flower is home grown

if grown up by her hands and how
green fingers and muddy elbows make up
gardening lands.

Write how Home is her.
And all the whimsical whistle stop tropes of a hope for a future
in Tesco's carrier bags.

Home is for every nag of fag butts on window sills,
and the lag of internet connection bills.

And I write this from a keyboard.
With Home's arms wrapped around my neck,
like infrastructure.

Orchestra

Hi.
I know, it's been a while.
I'm sorry.
I can't walk through this door
like the walls around the frame aren't crumbling

So I'll just stand here. With my toes on the rug.
So you know that I'm home
but I'm two heel taps from a hurricane.

The truth is
I'm scared. No, scratch
that.
I'm terrified.
Frozen in place and time
like a Roman clay statue
because I can never move
on from you.

When I'm scared, my body
is an orchestra.
I hold a quiver in my vocal
chords
that strums me like a verbal
acoustic guitar.
It plucks, speeding up stutters and stumble word
flutters
as I start to tell you
I'm starving for you.

My body is percussion. My heart is a bass drum.
That paces my race from this spot
with my toes in the doorway.

My lungs are the cymbals.
That symbolise the clattering when
I couldn't breathe you in, I breathe you out.
Pushing drumstick lumps in my throat
that spout out my doubt.

My body is a piano. With keyboard tiles for feet,
I run up scales
of minor dedication and major anxiety
landing on a fourth cadence consequence.
My body is an orchestra.
And you.
You're an unfinished song.

My anxiety hums inside of me
like a continuous attempt
to Heimlich manoeuvre a hymn from you.
Get you singing again.

The truth is, I'm scared.
No scratch that. I'm petrified.

Because you are the bag of marbles I used to call
mental health illnesses.
But you have grown so far beyond that
you are the pillow I rest my head onto.

You have mirrors taped over my eyes
so I can see all the ways I looked at you.
All the angles that were your best.
All adjacent to my hypotenuse.

Despair is just a fancy word for being tired
And darling, I am so tired.

I lay flowers at your feet and kiss your cheek of
cobblestone.
Hi. I know,
it's been a while. I'm sorry.
I can't walk to this grave
like the walls around the frame aren't crumbling.

  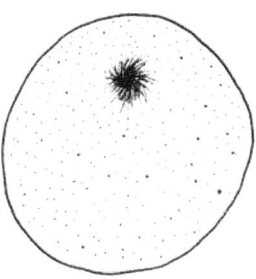

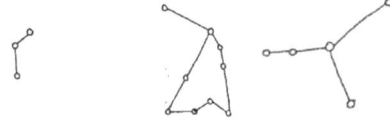

Home is not a choice

I see bodies stretched out
like paint lines and hate crimes
that look a lot like drawings making love.

I see you. Standing with your knees bent.
Ready for flight because alighting this world feels
just, easier.

Your crime was locking her eye into locking her
lips into locking down feelings because padlocks
are heart shaped.

You have never liked how men look back at you.
That smile they muster, musk cologne that's
sticking to their collar,
must have been too strong because you crave
perfume.

The fumes of citrus fruits, soft lips lining fruit
bowls
you are a fruit loop. Bold and daring.
You are wearing hoop earrings. Upon hearings
of the body he once touched
You were dressed like a slut. Why wouldn't you
want him.

Darling, I have scanned the corners of a rainbow
flag until
it's every sunset I can sink a dream into.

You are gay.
This mirror is glass
and you are shallow,
shallow waters.

And as you punch this mirror the shards
of a girl you once saw will scatter in blossoms
into an aisle seat. Watching a show of a girl
you could only have dreamed to be.

Paint your skin in red lips
and green dresses.

Paint your dreams in green slips
and red apples
Newton - maybe something will fall for you.

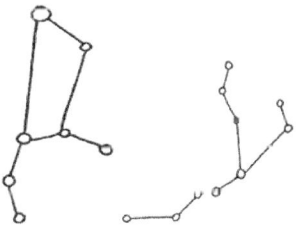

Sunflowers on skirting boards

I never write happy love poetry.
Because to me the saddest art
is the only part I can press to paper planes.

I'll write tales of break ups like they make up
the foundation on my skin and those who kiss it.
I'll paint pictures with monotone shades.
Running strokes across Heartaches
like an unseen tomorrow is my yesterday,

and now?
Now I am out of sad words.
Like a cascade of silent nightmares
leave blank pages around my feet.

Because now,
all I can think about,
is the way she holds her coffee cup.
The way she lifts up each quiet night
with louder smiles and quicker heartbeats.

It's been a while. Since my solemn pained membrane
could form chains of happy lexical fields
but these chains resemble daisies.
And she?
She's the fingers at the end of the playground
Tying up flowers to guide me home.
She's a tightrope typewriter

I can never fall off as
she trampolines back to a cloud nine
She is a Jenga tower on first dates.
Using building blocks to block out our next words
like stumbling bricks are our preamble.
Like fumbling fingers is a keyboard typing out
Sonnets.
Like mumbling lips curve round words and knock
down gender brick barriers.

She is sunflowers on skirting boards.
For every time I punch on kitchen walls
for a better world
she is the seam of the house running with prettier
Sunday's.

She blossoms.
Entwining kind smiles and fast heartbeats
to show me there is a better week ahead

I never write happy love poetry.
But darling, you are the first ink line of a better life
and I beg of you to show it to me.

Fridge magnets

There was a note on my window this morning.
Not on my fridge, no.
You never made it into the house.
Your quick escape left my drapes
soaked in rain that draped   draped
        draped
over my eyelids

The note said   I want you.
But what part of skimming rocks
across my heart could make you say
you want to

I am a paper mâché persona.
Of the girl you made me into.
Paper Mashed into the passion
you called love and affection
well I struggle to see how love can mean
destruction.

And sometimes I don't recognise your face, no,
because that smile is not the one from our first
kiss.
Your cheeks don't curl the way they did
when we sat in trollies with broken brollies
because the weather was too rough to handle.

And I lit candles in the places we once loved

to ignite the warmth of your skin
It didn't work   didn't work   didn't
work because

There's a mortality in existence
But immortality in your essence, in a sense
I can take your face in my pillow case. Even now I have to face that
the sparks died the way your pride
withered without watering

It didn't work   didn't work
didn't work because
There's a morality in caring but
Immorality in daring, racing hearts that raced from my window leaving a note.

When I read it again it said "I need you". Well, I need you too.
But not in a love way. More in the day
where we skip the mundane hey, to the stinging goodbye.

I let us die.
But that isn't because your breathing made my skin itch
or your panting made my toes twitch
We died because you made us brief.

And it's a relief to know
I locked my window

to your paper note
so you can't tear my coat of loneliness.
We shut the doors. To impermanence.

Bluebird

I walked in on her trimming down her wings.
She said a girl at school had called her feathery.
The bluebird used to tell me of the songs tucked in her backpack.
But she'd never unzip it.
The bluebird talked of many times she'd sat staring at the chalkboard wondering how such a blackness could be filled
And I would ask if she was alright.

Yeah, I'm fine. Just trying to find tomorrow.

The bluebird never ate lunch.
Tucked bread into her rib cage and pretended it was digested
but we all saw her pocket trailing breadcrumbs to the bathroom.
Fingers down her gullet.
The bluebird buried her stomach in a toilet bowl that asked if she could see straight.

Yeah, I'm fine. Just trying to find tomorrow.

The bluebird laughed at jokes about the world falling to ruin

Would dye her head feathers flurries of pink,
would think of rockstars as family because
family locked the living room door two weeks
ago.
The bluebird listens to Pink on full volume
while the walls vibrate their secrets
in a language bluebird only knows as pain.
In the morning. Egg cracks.
Toaster dings.
Coffee splashes on placemats, mums moan and
dads tut.
But there's no music today.
The mother feels it first in the stomach she's
been faking feeding
but we can all see the breadcrumbs in her pocket,
Leading to the bathroom.
The bluebird had buried her future.
In a bathtub with a note, written with trembling
pens.
Pens that will never write again.
And it read.

Yeah, I'm fine. Just trying to find tomorrow.

Dying of the light from electric fish tanks

Sometimes I wonder why my parents fought the way they did.
I knew an argument by the pillows placed crooked on a sofa
small enough for a neck ache but big enough to hold
the space in conversations about dad.
I knew an argument like a candle being blown out to be lit
while the smoke starts to climb from wasted breath.
I found wasted tears in the kitchen sink
left for the cat to drink.
Milk is for a sunny day and all we have is rain
they'd say
and laugh quietly, throwing away
the last of the dinner scraps.
I knew an argument by the back track of words on the conveyor belt of a tongue
and how they sounded when they had overrun.
I sucked my lollipop tongue till I was ten
to try to dry the words that steady
Alphabet spaghetti
Spilling out sad in *where's dad*
and when will you find the potato smiles?
I know an argument like a sorry that starts the sentence.
By the comedy of anger

and the anger of the laugh that came from fear.
I knew a fist bang to a table and the table to say sorry.
I knew a tap to run but never leave the kitchen.
I knew a black cat to cry over pasta.
I knew a smile that sunk through sofa cushions faster than
the dying of the light from electric fish tanks.

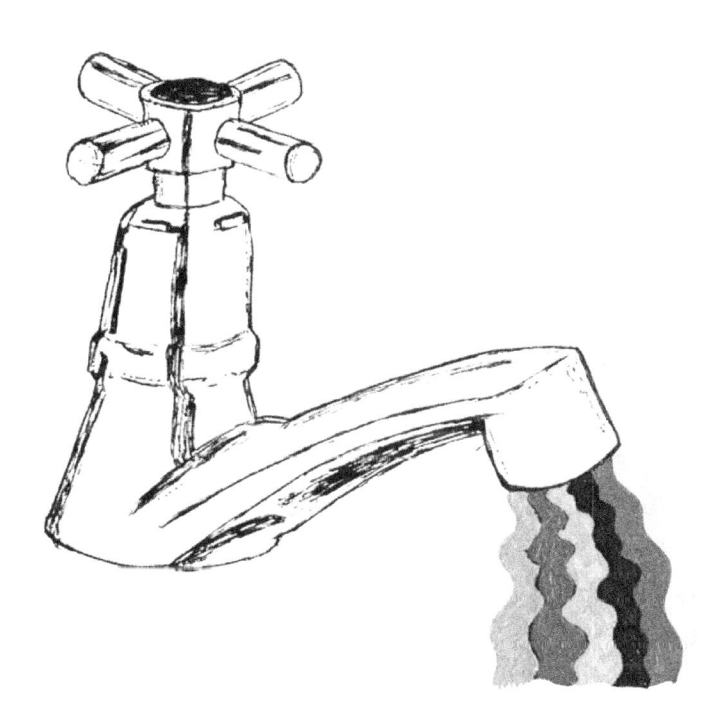

I've grown accustomed to the idea of silence on my tv screen

I've seen it sit there saying it'll try again tomorrow
just to stumble onto morning
mourning absence of its yawning static touch.
Bleeding yellow.

I've grown accustomed to the idea of static love.
The part after explosions
when the world is holding breath
staring at breakfast
breaking faster in their cars.

I am sitting in the moment where we ended.
I've put my shoes on the rug by the door.
I've left the metre running between my laces.
They know I won't be far behind them.
I've tucked my keys into my pillowcase
so when I sleep I know I'm faced with where I'm standing.

And on that bed there is you and I.
Frozen in time
growing mould

bodies turned cold with the climate.
We are stagnant water tired of tripping over itself
treading on each other's toes.

We are the drowning of woes,
the deteriorating clothes,
the showcase in a jumpsuit
a prison of our minds and no,

I do not wish for it to end.
I only wish for it to play out.
To become a song we all know about but no
longer stuck in our heads.
To be a tv programme cancelled
Leaving a screen sitting still in a living room
leaving room for me
To breathe.

I've grown accustomed to the idea of silence on
my tv screen.
    I've grown accustomed to the idea of silence.

FRUIT SALAD AND ROCKET SHIPS

CHAPTER TWO: Love letters Left in Orbit

Time: 23:00
Location: RA 17h 45m 40.04s,
Dec −29° 00' 28.1"
Feeling: Queer

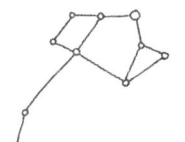

Papillon climbs back into their tinfoil rocket. Their suit is stained with pinks and blues, but now it feels as though the colours had always been there, waiting to be painted. A warm feeling bubbles in Papillon's stomach, as the rocket ship burns apples, and begins its journey back towards the darkness.

I will reach Hope. I will burn an orchard just to make it there on time.

Back floating amongst the stars, Papillon is daydreaming. As the night gleams chance and luck and future, Papillon is dancing their mind in the shadow between the star's light when suddenly, a sheet of paper covers Papillon's line of sight.

Stopping their travels abruptly, Papillon dons a paper suit and steps out into the blanket of black surrounding the ship.

This feels like breathing.

On the front of the ship lies a piece of paper, torn at the edges, worn at the words.

This is a love letter.

Confused and yet curious, Papillon sees a trail of sheets discarded along the darkness, forming a milky way of memories, too soft to be thrown away, too hard to be lost.

Papillon begins to read.

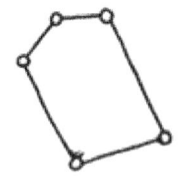

Paris in the stars

I say there's magic in our skin
she says
there's stardust in your hair.
And she brushes it
like I graze my
hand in dew
in the morning
and it is
summertime with
her.

I say there's
wizardry in the
bliss that breeds
itself
between the
making love of our
palms.
She says
*I will hold your
hand in the rain.*
And I swear
I am sitting on a tidal wave,
boat umbrella bounding towards rooftops.
She is holding the brolley gear stick in one hand,

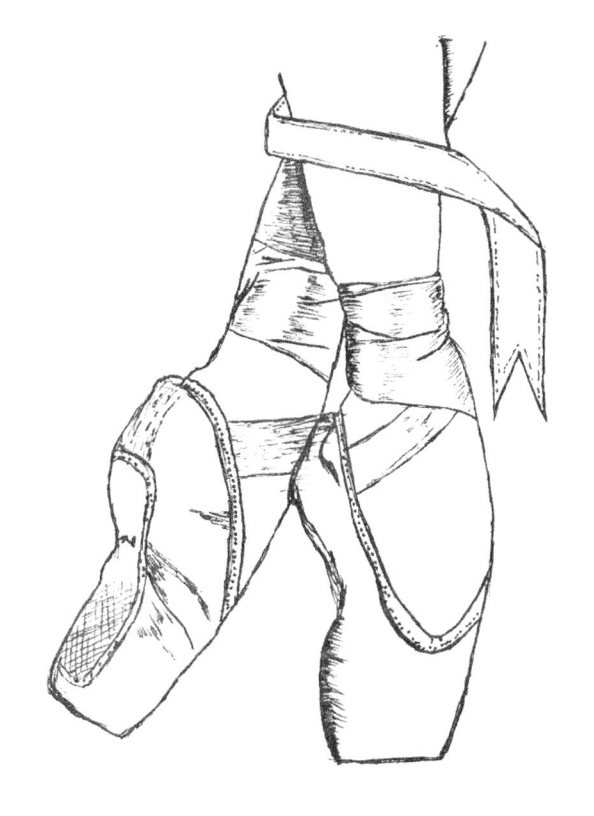

drawing circles on the inside of my palm in the other.

I say there's magic in our cupboard
and she raises her eyebrows.
A slight smile says she's translated the language of love
found in Parisian nights that last a little longer.

She is Paris in the stars.

She is downstairs in the living room,
Arguing with technology,

And I hear Paris call me by name.

And leaves a postcard beside my bed frame.

The Rainbow Archive

Welcome to The Rainbow Archive.

The hottest place to meet singles

Of the same derived sexual preference.

User number 34557

Asterisk, lost heart.

Name?

Alice Rose.

Height?

Well I haven't grown since year nine so I'd say

Five foot five.

Weight?

Between a feather and a hard place.

Wait, what weight?

Not applicable.

Pet hate?

People who open messages and leave without a response.

I SEE you.

Have you got any Interests?

Chasing sunsets until my ankles fall off

or chasing ice cream vans until their wheels fall off

or chasing butterflies until my wings fall off-

In short; "likes running"

Favourite food?

Broccoli.

It is the green goddess of the land

And we can grab it

from every corner shop

stacked like disciples

I worship every tender stem tree I can climb.

In short, "likes broccoli"

What's your deepest most kept secret?

I have more stuffed animals than friends.

Thank you Alice, for sharing your truth.

Last but not least, we just need to know

Why you? **Why you?**

Because

we could dance like catapults.

We could kiss the sun if she smiled at us.

We could climb the sky like a rope swing, tugging on the fabric of time or the fabric of her skirt, whichever seems more wondrous.

And we could laugh at hyenas who roll their shoulders and shake their eyes

and we could chase the morning.

We could snooze the day.

We could tell the skipping rope that play

is losing your breath in the middle.

Losing second chances.

Losing second glances and

learning to look at lost things like experiences,

we could have it all.

I loved her enough to be happy for her.

Waving to the back of her head.

Leaving me here

filling the space between text boxes,

boxing up memories she tossed aside like

broccoli stems.

Cradling stuffed bears baring the emptiness

in my pothole of a chest.

So if you are to love me,

love me keeping you up at night singing songs from the seventies.

Love the me who cries in kitchens.

And the me who changes the lids to pens

to make the reveal more exciting.

Love me like she never could.

Love me like I'm something.

Thank you for registering.

We look forward to finding you love.

User 34557

Asterisk - lost heart.

Valentine with wool for eyes

14th of February. 14, 02, XX.

I fill the XX with the ex I will see this day with.

Cut my calendar into heart shapes of paper to play with

making aeroplanes that would reach out to your palms.

But reality has a harsh way

of taking planes of plain old loving and making them loathing

Because in reality,

I am all the parts you don't see in her.

I fill the cracks in your paving stones

like the bones of who I am are chopped up

to make your perfect girl.

But you keep her there. Porcelain face and blonde ish hair

unaware that she's only one
puzzle piece.

Muzzled me sinks into

pieces thinking

she will never know she's not
enough for you.

14. 02. XX.

I am only a moment.

A component to slide in the fingertips

of what she couldn't reach for.

We are a marriage of two tongues laced with secrets

promising they won't let the other slip

14 02 XX.

This is my anti-Valentine's Day landmine.

Step on the words the way you stepped over her

like there are trip signs

Taste the starters. This is just the beginning.

You were winning. Had your arms pinning down two maps

because we were two separate worlds. At least we were

till I learnt how to fly,

with my aeroplane high,

through the thumb print cracks in your thighs,

and looked down to see her in your eye.

14 02 XX.

I stopped breathing.

Though you never let me catch air

and pump it into my lungs

because my tongue was always latched to your leaving.

Somehow I still stopped breathing.

I watched two bodies I thought I'd known pass by my own

into sunsets when I'd yearned for moonlight.

You   broke
       me.

Into   pieces of
    poetry.

So here is your poem.

Built up with line breaks to requiems,

prose to propose I'm as worthy as them

I have words tucked tenuously,

stuck between fingernails and the skin you touch,

they claw at me.

Slipping themselves silently

into the art you can clutch.

You hold me arms length

Shoulder width apart

Your eyes, as they dart to the ceiling.

Unfeeling. Untouched.

14, 02, XX.

Now there's nothing to say but; next.

When you arrive

When you arrive, put the kettle on.
Know that I'm gonna need a fix
as asphyxiating
as the flicks of you.

Put the kettle on. Brew up a bridge
we can cross with crossed eyes
crossing a room to each other

When you arrive, I won't be breathing.
I'll be too busy leaving
my mind on the mantle
mentally meeting
you

Because you are the seething coffee pot
that whistles to bring me closer.

You are the melted biscuit
I left to soak
for a toke too long in between smokes
because I couldn't risk it distracting us.

When you arrive, know that I've already left.
I have run the streets screaming your name
like a bird's morning chirp.
I have perturbed
every street passer

with hazy glasses
with fast spoken words
of have you seen this girl

When you arrive, I have met you three times over.
Sketching out in my mind
every freckle you've covered
with thick scarf secrecy

and each idea you haven't even said yet.
When you arrive, know we've already met.
And kiss me, like it's in debt.

The coping strategy

1. Wake up every afternoon.
Remember that the morning was when you had breakfast;
when she'd roll into your pillow
and cushioned your waking into a better day.
Know that sleeping until the afternoon
ensures your cereal won't taste soggy,
make sure your morning without her never exists.

2. Drink until you can't see her eyes.
The ones you locked in slow dances
and mapped out chances of kisses on your bed sheets.
Drink until pain feels like
jäger shots and sour afternoon throw ups

3. Text her every evening.
Her words will cut like glass shards
caressing unkissed skin.
When she says leave,
swear you'll leave your phone unlocked
for when she takes those words back

4. Download a new game
Distract yourself with monotone pixels
and aimless goals.

Because where will life go if goals
aren't going to higher levels and playing again.

5. Do all you can to feel whole.
You will become a cavern of self torture,
A slaughterhouse
for only after thoughts.
They will haunt
your Thursday evening to your Wednesday morning,
taking cigarette breaks where you think you feel better.

6. Chase her until your legs start aching.
Run down streets you used to walk down
embrace your shin splints
splinter your ankles
tell her you miss her like it's streaked
in cartoon shows behind you.
Because I miss you will linger
on memory lane like a perfume streak.

7. Love her until she stops breathing.
Love for her is six feet deep
and never quite gets easier.
Pillows feel lumpy,
alcohol replaced the morning coffee
a long time ago.
Know that the air will run out so long as the pillow

stays stuck - taped to your face.
Know that the love will run out so long as the love
never came in the first place.

Please don't make me your next supernova

I have time bombs tied to my wrists that tick
every time I tell you I love you.
They laugh like they know the joke but never say
the punch line
until I punch time in that stop watch for the
minute I saw our love die in your eyes.

I can see a supernova. You dress me in purple
and rose tint my red flags to pink
and the stars are giants balls of fire
I will burn you on impact.

To my Icarus.
My wide hearted dancer of the space between
our hands
when you touch me I will explode.

When you touch me I will implode into myself
Fragmenting I love you with I'm singing to your
ears.
A song I didn't write but I will
acoustic cover my heart for you.

My feelings are mirrored glass. Tinted windows.
I watch you Icarus, dancing with your shoes off.
You are naked and I am wearing armour.

You say I look beautiful in the reflection,
I see a girl deflecting kindness for a battle ground
and I stab you with a sorry, straight through the
soft bare chest
you had trusted me with.

The red of my supernova is the beating hearts of
the body partially breathing in my hands.
I will call your name like a battle cry.
Icarus, I will never let the sky forget you.

Jazmine

Jazmine was a dancer.
She would prance her fingertips on the
hearts of the men that would pass her.

With serpent eyes Jazmine hypnotised
every new brewed star crossed lover.

Jazmine conjured up a fairytale. Laying down
carpets
like she could be your gravity.
Floating off like you and me
could touch the fabric lining of reality.

In the dark,
Jazmine rubbed on lamps that spouted gold dust.
Made you see genies while she grasped your
neck,
a choke hold in a mould she told you was love.

She swallows you whole.

And in your drunk pink tinted chamber
you think that the hole she's left
is a whole new world.

You rim it with thoughts of a better life.
Jazmine watches the thoughts grow bitter from
better

and slips opium into apple cores.

She is Eve when Adam is a street boy thiev-ing
like he could steal her heart for safe keeping.

Jazmine laughs. And starts to force feed him.
Speeding through his veins
until he starts bleeding
Jazmine laughs.
Says she'll never be his Eden.

FRUIT SALAD AND ROCKET SHIPS

CHAPTER THREE: Hope is a black hole

Time: 00:00
Location: NGC7727
Feeling: Absent

Papillon sinks back into the shape of the cardboard rocket ship. They choose to keep one letter. They will never say which one.
As Papillon travels deeper into the empty space between stars, a familiar feeling starts to peel like oranges turned rotten in their stomach.

Something is wrong.

The star named Hope is no closer than ten minutes prior. Papillon starts to decipher that Hope may not be on the horizon and calls themself a liar. A pain starts to transpire and a rage from waiting and contemplating their life begins a fire that burns the cardboard ship into a fragment of last minutes. Papillon is crying alone in the dark of an empty midnight. Their way home, their way to Hope, is flying in all directions, drifting cardboard parts discarded into

darkness. Fruit is losing its breath, rotting in the violence of nothingness and
Papillon.
Just.
Blinks.

Up ahead, Papillon notices a black hole growing nearer. It is in this moment that all begins to make sense. The light of Hope has never grown nearer. It is the ghost of light dimming slowly inside the black hole's open mouth, wide and growing. It looks like it has teeth. It looks like it is smiling.
Papillon.
Just.
Blinks.

As the tie between the hole and them runs thin, the broken bits of ship begin to elongate in the dark, sinking into the hole ahead of them. There is no time to run. There is no Hope to spark a light. Hope begins to feel like a myth told by mothers to make you dream. Papillon's ship is ripped at the seams, and all seems to be lost.

How dark it can be, when you don't believe in stars.

This is the story of Daniel the space man

There were glass walls stabilising universes.
Danny was the hammer,
shattering the spaces between
what could be, and what will never happen.

Danny was a traveller. Sliding between future me's
and past time you's

to calibrate untrodden ultimatums.
Danny has a delirium.

Whisper self taught
teachers
that don't get his
continuum
in parent meetings.

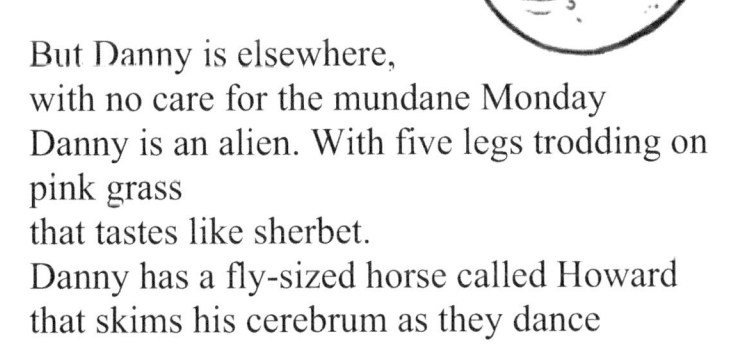

But Danny is elsewhere,
with no care for the mundane Monday
Danny is an alien. With five legs trodding on
pink grass
that tastes like sherbet.
Danny has a fly-sized horse called Howard
that skims his cerebrum as they dance

threw the cranium and onward.

When the bottle breaks knuckles in the kitchen.
The stars are where Danny's mind lives.
The light flickers lightyears and
flutters on his eyelids.
He's a kid.

But there's a sparkle in space
that has vacated retinas
when blankets are barricade defences.

This is the story of Daniel the space man.

Not a space boy, Dan is a man
when he learnt that man can be mean
Dan paid for the beans on his son's plate.

Dan has a crate. Of the "kids toys"
meant for little boys
that his wife has grown to hate.
But dan hides in the attic,
looks at the blink black breathing
of the places he can fabricate.

Dan hops on the nearest galaxy. Running rocks
in his fingers
that linger in circle currency.
Dan launches into alternate reality.

Where the tongue tied twelve year old
never told that girl that he was in love.

But by now,
the attic is broken down
and she's there with his rocket in pieces.

This is the story of Daniel the space man.
Where the universe
looks better
than the life he had to plan.

Where the stars
look so much brighter
than the future he's to span.

This is the story of Daniel the space man.
Because the world was too heavy to withstand.

Sorry, what did you say?

We're sitting at a bar.
I have my arm resting on the ledge.
She is telling me of the legislation of

We're sitting at a bar.
I can see coasters laughing in the corner.
I can hear a glass chiming
filled to the brim with a new good memory

Alice.

Alice.

Alice.

We're sitting in a classroom.
The teacher waves a pen at the squiggles she calls education
at the front.
I take the squiggles. Watch them
live and die in my mind.
Watch them peel from the board
and piggy back off of each other
out of the window

I have a textbook left on a cloud.

FRUIT SALAD AND ROCKET SHIPS

                                                          Alice.

                    Alice.

Alice.

We're sitting in a classroom.
The pen is pointing plainly
at a whiteboard without words.
But I can't tell her they were stolen.

                                                          Alice.

                    Alice.

Alice?

We're sitting in a living room.
People are playing tennis with their mouths.
I can see sounds paint the walls
the current climate changing on the thermostat,
the new born baby becoming a stage play of photographs
With no interval

                                                       Alice.

                    Alice.

ALICE!

You zoned out again.

ALICE!
Can you please focus on the work.

ALICE!
You know what. Never mind.

I'm just a floating meteorite

Directionless.
Colliding with planets
who apologise for the change in their oceans.
I wave goodbye before they can tie a satellite to
my meteorite body.
And make me see for them.
Make us part of the same gravity.
I am far too free
to stay in solar systems,
pay rent to a star
that I'll critique on Facebook for its policies.
I'm just a floating meteorite.
Directionless.
Wishing I'd never crashed into her life.

Office mornings

Clock. Water. Desk. Light.
I overthink the thought I had last night
when thinking thoughts is food and I'm a midnight snacker.
I take a whack at
seeing from your point of view
when you told me that she told you
that I'm not good enough for you,
when thinking thoughts like drinking I'll have some

water. Desk. Light. Clock.
And I investigate a mass of minds: a flock,
when minding how I breathe
is company's new policy
in company of you.
I sit silently with you,
Fully aware that each spin of my chair could result
in a molten hot glare I slip under the

desk. Light. Clock. Water.
I feel like a pig for the slaughter. Torn, tort, drawn and quartered
with each thought a stab here

I need you. Dear. To hear me clear
as I fear hearing clear is cheery to think
but for thought to appear
I turn on the

light. Clock. Water. Desk.
I wanted you to know I tried my best.
Sometimes I was underdressed to address my
mental health
and so sometimes I digress from us.

Because trust is hard
when lust is a windswept leotard,
hard to catch.

Because us is hard when the latch
clings me to the thinking all night
and the drinking until I hear the
clock. Water. Desk. Light.

Here we go again. Into the night.

The face of war (to rent)

I want to use my tears as paint
so that maybe you can see what makes me sad.

I have air caught in my lungs.
It feels like my mouth is a butterfly net and I am catching your
glances like lovebugs.
I chew them down into my stomach and the kick
as if I am their mother but spare me the family resemblance.

You have made me love you with your hair tied up.

You have filled my stomach like a garden.

There are stinging nettles hugging my legs.
They feel like letting go will hurt more.

I want to use my tears as paint
so I can at least make them useful.
Dampen my paint brushes.
Dampen my hot flushes,
cramp in my hands telling me

This poem is finished.

The testimony of a stage-hand

She had to treat me bad to treat her next lover better.
And this bitter buttercup just sits batting her big black lashes
like fighting the lack of big blue teardrops raining behind them.
Those were my eyes.
I learnt to swim.
Sit atop an upturned umbrella,
unlearned her mistakes,
prayed she'd lavender her choices,
look for a greener road to take.
But it was her mistake upon me to make
marking learning curves into my hips where her hands were, flaking at my sides.
Dressing me in sorry that seemed to sit like silk,
Slip me through her figures, I was just
the bit before the fix.
The crash course crashing, of course
into the fuck yous that looked like shores
and I'm sure she's lovely now.
That's how it goes when you finally float alone.
And with that, test dummies take bows from the wings of the stage.

The spotlight shines on the smile that hid the frowns,
we who bow in the shadows or windows to the person who gets
all the sunshine now.
Broken Barbie dolls with bruised artery holes. With love we'll be
holding them peacefully, together in holy matrimony.
The degree in the cold.
Qualified to hold the door open.

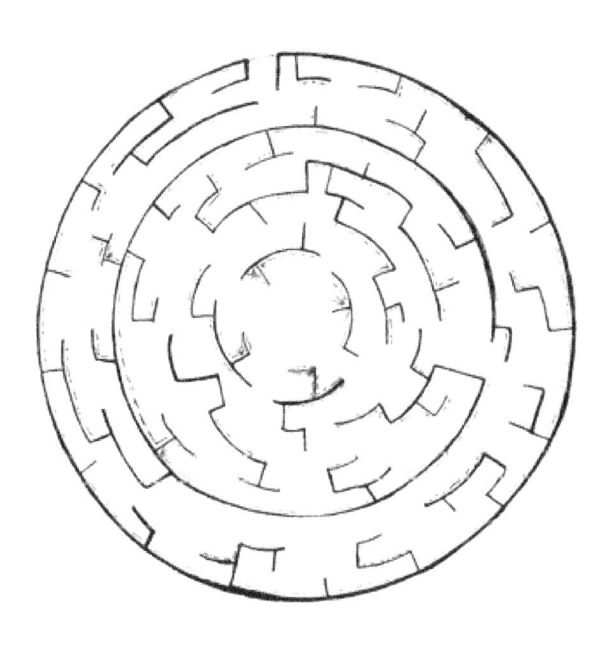

The hurricane

The door was left ajar as the sun started to fall between the trees.
She watched as the sunshine closed its eyes
and the night time awoke. Piercing the sky with a silent whiteness that
could only be described as a retreat flag.

The hurricane started small.
Crept under the carpet and tugged it slightly as she walked
through the house to the kitchen.
The hurricane danced through the pots and pans
flipping handles so they never landed
in her palms as she tried to cook.

The hurricane knocked down one book.
It opened to a page about self love.
She closed it. Put it back on the shelf she couldn't quite reach.

The night became brighter as the stars started staring at the house.
Maybe they could see the storm coming.

The hurricane started tumbling larger things from place.
With fumbling fingers she would space out objects in the prospect
They were stronger apart.
The hurricane objected.
Started knocking down books one by one,
found a gun beneath a cardboard
that had come with the house.

The hurricane danced across the living room.
Flipped over cushions to the side with the stain
she had tried to desperately hide and
she felt the rain begin to fall on her cheeks.
She wondered why she hadn't got a forecast today.

The night time starts to look like dot to dot,
as the stars spot problems in the wind.
They connect thoughts between their light and try
to guide her from the house.

The girl closes her curtains.
She thinks it's fine without the light
that so desperately tried to save her.
The hurricane is breathing now.

Slamming doors and counting down
kitchen timers. Making loud in what was once
a safe house.
The hurricane knows no bounds as it tears
wallpaper from itself,
peeling like lemons.
The girl holds a bitterness in her mouth.
Starts to lose sight of love and how
the sky looked.

Citrus. She sits as
the hurricane flips chairs and
chucks a fork in the microwave.

Brave. The girl begs to be saved
from the zoo that she has concaved herself into.

The hurricane takes the words from her mouth
and turns them into air.
She is silent now. Scared, so stuffs sentences
into a poem.

The dawn begins to creep between the gaps in
the curtains.
The light flashes blue, then red, then white.
The hurricane begins to flight, finding defeat
in the siren sky that begs the girl to stay inside.

When the air became still,
and the will to move had met the legs that carried her,
the girl began to piece together her home.
Stood chairs ready for guests
with kind eyes to sit in.
Balanced the pots and pans
in cupboards that closed a little too loudly.
Wiped the floorboards from the rain that puddled
in the street of the seat to the living room.
Put the book of self love onto a lower shelf.
Made it reachable.

And then,
when the house felt zen enough
to be home again,
she took a seat with the book, crossed feet and dried eyes.

And as she read the words to never open the door to hurricanes,
she hears the wind knocking against the window panes.

The door ajar. The sun has fallen down again.

FRUIT SALAD AND ROCKET SHIPS

CHAPTER FOUR: Home drive

Time: 00:30
Location: 22h 1m 38.39s -7° 15' 9.4"
Feeling: Peace

It is easy to find dust harder to clean once it's settled. To find darkness to be comfortable once darkest, to accustom your mind to mindlessness, to accept that less is all you will find.

But when you have found the lowest point, the only way forwards is up.

With a deep breath that felt like catapults in their chest, Papillon refused to accept that this was their story. That hope had been a fever dream and that they were not meant for glory. With this, Papillon sealed the hole in their suit with the letter that they had plucked from the stars. They thought of all the moments where love was art, where hope was a part of them that dreamed, where sun was not a burning star but the heart that beat in their chest. Papillon thought of the best way to make pain into passion. Dying into flying. Violence into silence and silence into loud. Papillon made themselves proud with the will to live happily alone amongst a crowd of sadness.

I am Here.

Not to scale

Jane Doe has one new post.
But it's not what you thought, no,
her tummy is tucked
cropped under her top and her jeans.

She is lean to get likes
but she eats up the comments.

In her head, she's a whale.
But to me, the only whale relativity
is the mammoth about of beauty
I see in her heart.

Jane Doe has been bullied to parts.
scattered through screenshots and you look hot's,
driven to cut herself out of the picture.

And John Doe has one new video.
Of him holding a pillow, the feathers spread out
on the floor.
John Doe is a case.
A pillow case.
Like a comfort ripped from its self love and place

He is sweet and petite but he cries because tweets
are not little birds chirping sweet lexis.
They are crows in disguise.
feeding lies to young minds

but you.
You are unequivocally beautiful.

You short, or thin,
skin, or bone,
you are home in the body you build.

You are a temple.
Worship each rock that is thrown
and make it your walls.

You are a fighter.
You got up today.
Threw on your clothes.
Prepared for the hey hoe or slag though
You dared to be brave.
Turn away from the mirror. Because you don't need to look.
Just look at the skin of your paperback book and remember.

You made it here.

I'm still in love with you

Not in a way that
I'll leave breadcrumbs at your door
for you to find me again,

Or that I'll leave my door open to see
the hallway darkened by your shadow.

Just in a way that
it spills out in poems when I make
the coffee you like.
Or that I smile at how my name
drips from your tongue
like you make honey in the beehive
of your stomach.

Or that my stomach swirls like chocolate
at the curl of the letters
that pen out I love you
in an old letter left
in the drawer I never touch.

I won't be the one to hold your shoulder blades
during a thunderstorm.
Or the towel to keep you dry and warm
after baths in candlelight
with blades in bathroom cupboards
that seem less sworn to danger
when your eyes are worn and weary.

Or the one to put on cheer me up
buttercup lyrics
buttering your toast in an afternoon
sea of tea
and brown sugar cubes
and brown paper bags
full of takeaway food

because for me,
you took the sun away from my windowsill.
Unpicked the seams of my trust
like an unworn skirt
that you used to love.
Swirling like chocolate.

Breathing through paper bags
trying to stop the thunderstorm
clapping a chorus in my head.
Instead, I am unsung lyrics in a bed
you've never touched before.

But you hum the tune as you kiss her neck
and percussion her waist with your fingers.

I will linger inside your yesterdays.
As a song, you can't quite remember the name
of.

T-shirt

I hung you out to dry.
Put my puckered lip pegs
along your seam lines to hold you in place.

That morning, we played basketball.
Though the basket, granted
was actually a mud hole
and the ball was crumpled up crisp packets.

But with you,
the reality of back garden fragility
backed away from the forefront of my mind.
Instead I back track
to the line of your neck
when you first offered me hot cups of good
morning.

We shared our first sips of a new life
through rimmed lips that fold around the coffee
beans.

I ran across your body seams,
feeling each tie that
Connects your limbs
like ribbon trims.

We took a break from broken hole basketball
and I borrowed your jam and butter.
I spread across the slices of bread
Like starchy notepads with poetic words.

Because that unheard Wednesday sandwich
is the best poetry I have ever written.

Watching your mouth stuff my lines in
like a hungry art chipmunk
leaving breadcrumb trails of missing letters on
your fabric features.

I hung out your shirt today.
I thought you might want to collect it.

Saturn

1426, 666, 422.
Saturn sits in a rocking chair of hydrogen.
Gentle.
Old age like a kiss on lips
that lie lipless on the precipice of growing.
Her jewelleries the rage.
Rings ranging from 30 to 7
and voices from heaven asking where she got them from.

In her youth.
Saturn was a constantly rotating basketball hoop.
Running loop　　　　de　　　　　　loop
with discarded parts
of the art
　　　　　that she tore
　　　　　　　　　　apart
parting meteor　　　　　　　to metres
more
of dancing space

1426, 666, 422.
Saturn sits singing symphonies to the planets that will listen.

In her late orbit.
Saturn wore a boxing ring
tied around her waist
to waste no time with
touching   feeling   meteorite
Saturn made haste,
when big space
              spaces Saturn
                        from the sun
and sits her singing sixth away
                    at her own self
          fulfilling pace

1426, 666, 422.

Saturn sits staring blankly at the blackness
between stars.

She is shaped like spacecraft.
She is a crafted space shape,
a spacious shape shift
and a shapeless craft space
in a kids science drawer

Saturn has never asked you how your day was.
Simply sat there.
Recycling smiles

and wise well wishes
and she'll ask you to stay a while.

But in this interstellar nursing home
there's so much to see
and stretch out
                        and sketch out
                                              in
space maps and she

understands that.

But she has the moons.
Sixty two orbiting carers,
checking the glint in her cosmos cosmetics.

Saturn has a spacemaker taped to her chest
for each time that you tell her
she is the *best* planet
running rings round all the rest.

Saturn hasn't asked for a call in a decade.

                                            Ring
Saturn answers but never hangs up

                                      Ring
Saturn downs cups of stardust and laughs

                                      Ring
Saturn dances to the songs that we sing.

                                      Ring

Saturn.

1426, 666, 422.

A conversation with suicide

Sunshine
oranges
peppermint pillows,
green chasing grass
back door glass windows.

When I first met her I was
Six
     Six.
She told me
     Sunshine doesn't
     happen on its own
     time darling
When I first met her I said
What do you do to keep from shadows every day?

     Well honey,
  Don't you think the world is painted?

When I first met her, I was
Scraping my knees on new memories,
Falling in love with my palms and how they touch trees
passing in a playground I would never see again.

She said
baby,
I can show you evergreen.
Deep sea blue between
your eyes and the
bottom of a swimming pool
drown, baby.
Sink down to the mermaids,
ask for me.

When I first met suicide I was six years old.
She had rosy cheeks
But burnt eyes
She made cloudy lemonade
In my bathtub
She was so, damn,
beautiful.
I told her
I love you like a fire exit.
Like a big escape button
from the beating
And the everybody knows it
Brown nosing little shit
You'd better not come into school today.

Hospital blue and red stain my corneas.

I blink crazy from my eyes and sit with suicide in
a neat and sterile bed.
She says,

> *We were so close, baby.*

Suicide and I part ways and become pen pals.
I tell her when the world stops turning
I tell her why I should still be in it.
I tell her when her eyes are burning, blink twice
to fade from home.
And I tell her,
Let me write just one more poem.
Let me laugh just a little longer
Let me dance a little stranger
Let me cry about girls and love myself better
Let me live like I should have at six
Let me breathe just a little bit slower.

Kind hearts are made for bigger things than this.

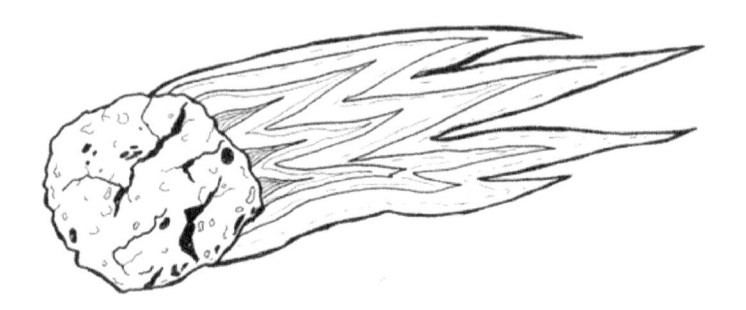

A ROCKY LANDING

Time: 01:00
Location: 51°07'34"N 1°18'03"E
Feeling: Grounded

Papillon squeezed their eyes shut and wished upon themselves to bring the ground back to their feet. They would not float in the dark and let defeat seep into their pores and get underneath their skin. Papillon would choose to fight. And Papillon would choose to win.

Papillon opened their eyes.

Grass hugged their toes. They could feel a cool wind blow through the trees. Neck hairs stood to attention. This was home as they knew it.

However, when Papillon looked to their tinfoil house, something was different. The house did not sink at the knees, but stood with ease to the air, breathing gently. Inside, though the fire had all but died, the young girl grew a smile as Papillon arrived, meeting their body with a hold that squeezes them just right. With two steps and a right, though there still boils a slow burning fight, it seems to simmer in delight. Papillon is faced with smiling eyebrows, raising lips and a warm embrace.

With three turns to the right, five steps and a look upwards, Papillon grazes the staircase to their purple door, left unopened. With the turning of the doorknob, Papillon fills their room with the warmth glowing from their chest. Their spacesuit is laid to rest, the letter placed by the mirror, and an apple facing the door.

Papillon crosses their legs, sitting upon the welcoming floor.

And with pen in hand, Papillon's mind begins to explore.

What have I been waiting for?

BONUS CHAPTER: THE POLKA-DOT SHOP (and other absurdities)

The Polka Dot Shop

Baths are full body sinks
or very small swimming pools.

It's funny how objects fall down when you're not looking.
Once you've gone.
Almost like they were too shy to not look strong for you.

There is a blue old shop in my hometown.
It has piles of crazy characters climbing out,
out of the polka dot front door.

You should eat green vegetables.
Or green through green glasses,
wear a matching handbag if you're feeling classy.

Dance forever. Dance your legs off.

Chests are just boobs
but on linked-in.

I like scrunchies.
Scrunchers.

They find themselves scrunching all day to get home
and elasticate. Relax till eight
when the clock chimes for a new episode of -

Hair bands. Hit music show.

The lamp outside
just said goodnight
through the front room window
that sticks out a bit.

The lamp looks like
a giraffe neck
and a garden of stories -

How do you increase water?
How do you multiply h2o?
When can you create water
rather than moving it from one place to another?

Can anything be made?
Is everything finite?
Expiry date stickers.

Corner shop security camera.
Capturing expired liquid made of rivers

and the shop walls quiver under the weight of it.
Capitalism in bottle caps.

Bottle caps look like birdseed
in a world that is hungry.
There are tummies that look
like
shopping baskets
basking in the sun
of some beach you only drove
past.

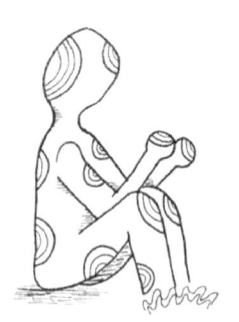

What if inverted colours of your favourite colour
are your least favourite colour?

Bubbles

POP
Neon glow.
Rounded windows.
Laughing chins,
clinking glasses
filled with

POP
Late goodbyes.
Early hellos.
Whispering eyelids,
washing liquids
covered in

POP
Gentle rooftops.
Dented pillows.
Breathing bookends
clapping pages
speaking of

POP

Purple endings.

Was it something in the waves that told you it
wasn't a beach day that day?

Bottle caps look like birdseed
in a world that's hungry.
There are tummies that look like
shopping baskets
basking in the sun
of some beach you only drove past.

Was it something in the waves that told you it
wasn't a beach day that day?

Have you ever stopped drinking hop from the
plastic,
picture the moment your hand,
pulls the polymer from the ethanol
pulls the wrapper from the beer
pulls the noose out of the wardrobe.

Some bird is gonna lose the right to breathe
today.
Have it snatched away by a couple of beers with
the lads.

Frogs hop through lily pads
like stepping stones to a better life.

Bigger dreams,
and brighter suns.

My period is a traffic light

My period is a traffic light.
When it stops running red I am green lit
to go get whatever I need to feel this
empty feeling. Fall to its knees.

I don't remember when I started stapling tissue
paper to my cheeks.
I guess I feared that crying
would mean I'd lose my hands in whatever
I'd be holding at that time,
and I would roll the toilet paper up my cheeks to
catch the rain.
because my brain is a black cloud
and I can't quite seem to find
the right words to entertain thunder.
It just rumbles.
In bellies.
Sick.

My period is a traffic light.
When it stops running red I am green lit
to starve myself again.
To cut peas in half and save them for tomorrow.
To tie dye my organs.
Changing the colour of my anatomy
with every illness I push myself towards
by being skinny, and scared.

I feel like an unprepared jacket ripping at the shoulders,
showing other coats
pictures from its holiday.
How this jacket got wasted
and danced under lamps
that told moths of politics.

How this jacket wandered roads
instead of pathways.
Wanting the traffic to come.

Periods are traffic lights,
when they stop running red I am
green lit to go.

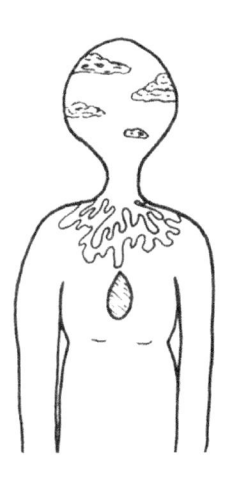

He said.

The jacket doesn't remember the rest.

Slightly torn and blurred.

The jacket drags itself to its doorstep.

Finds a hanger.

And stays there, saying it was just another rainy day.

FRUIT SALAD AND ROCKET SHIPS

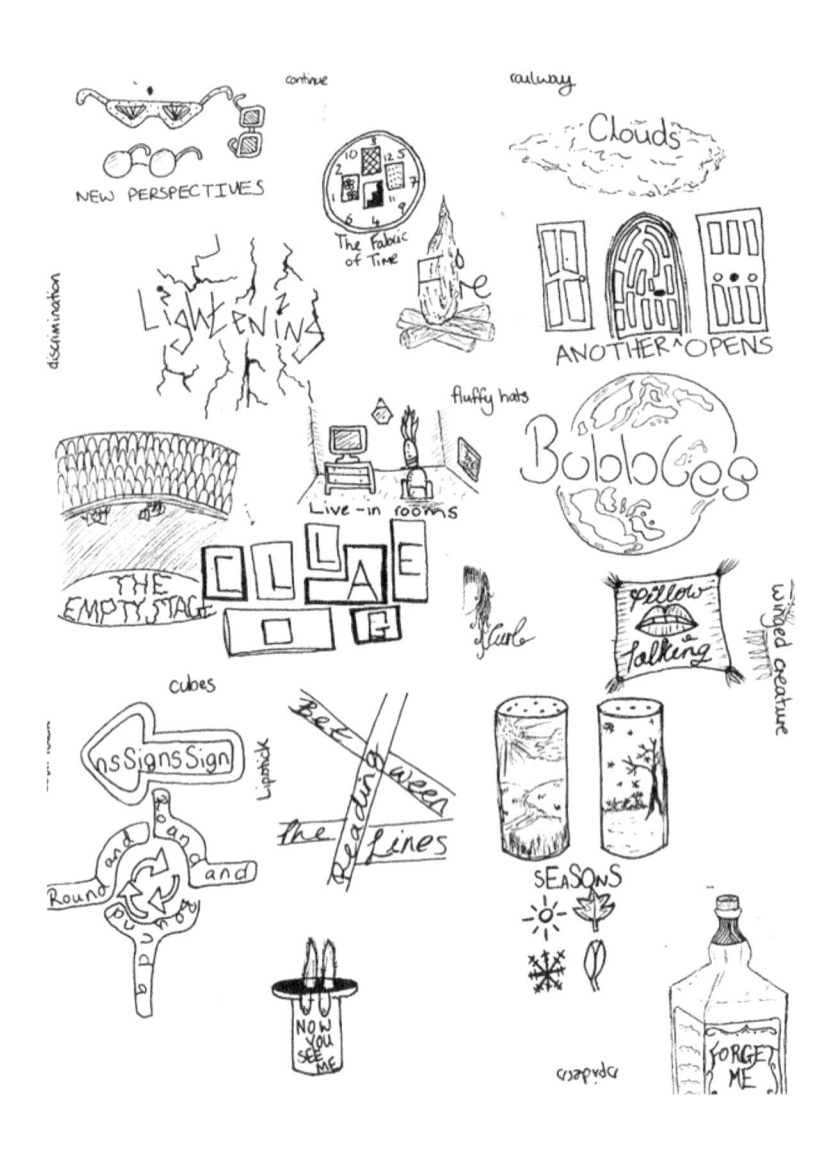

FRUIT SALAD AND ROCKET SHIPS

You have a story in your skull

That can never seem to leave it.
Let it sit at lunch with your family.
Talk about weather that never happened,
clouds you only made from the head that just
won't stop talking.
You try to paint a sky that's blue,
but you ran out of paint brushes.
The last time you let your brain tell you the truth

but you put on new shoes,
left the house one day
caught up with nature
as it ran away from you
panting to be treated
better
the leaves at your feet are tired.
They have been floating for such a long time.

You are weary and weak,
your arm fell asleep
when you told your hand *I will not scour my
body for sacrifice today*

But you know that being asleep just means
hitting pause on a programme you didn't realise

You were watching
until you look at the chair next to you.

How it carries no weight in its plush pink cushion.
How your soul has left you in the living room.
And now you cradle your frame like a promise.

The story behind the salad

The narrative behind 'Fruit Salad and Rocket Ships' is an autobiographical depiction of my battle with depression, love and trauma, both while growing up and while writing this book for the past five years.

Mirror house on the rainbow meteor
Coordinates: My hometown, Dover
As a child, I lived in a rainbow house; each room was painted a different colour, with a yellow kitchen, a yellow and green living room, orange bedroom, pink bathroom, blue toilet. I lived in the purple room. This rainbow home inspired the idea of home being this magical, rainbow place, but on another level, finding a rainbow home is closely linked to my journey of coming out as a lesbian. When I came out, gay marriage was still illegal, and I stayed closeted for a lot longer than I feel comfortable with. Accepting that I was queer and beautiful meant that I could find a body that I felt at home in, hence the rainbow meteor feeling both familiar and welcoming. If you are a young LGBTQ+ person navigating coming out, know that I am proud of you, and you will have such a massive queer family

welcoming you with open arms when you take that small step for mankind, and huge step for you!

Love letters left in orbit
Coordinates: The centre of the milky way
The love letters left in orbit are a myriad of love poems I wrote over the past seven years, spanning several people from my life. As poets, we often write of love and passion that transcends time. I wanted to create a conversation that paid respect to the love of yesterday, celebrating it as a piece of art that still orbits my world and made me who I am today..

Hope is not a place
Coordinates: The constellation of Aquarius, home of two black holes
As a child, I went through some extreme stages of grief, trauma and emotional development between the ages of 7 and 11, which inspired the character Papillon. As a teenager and now young adult, I went through bullying, assault and suicidal ideation, resulting in about 7 years of therapy and a plethora of mental health diagnoses. The premise of entering the cosmos is poems and a narrative of my personal experience with grief and struggle, losing my ability to

vocalise my emotions and feeling like I was drowning, unable to pull myself back to reality.

Home drive
Coordinates: The real star from this book (see next page)
Home drive is exactly what it says on the tin. In the duration of writing this book, I have developed the strength, courage and drive to bring myself out of the darkness I coated myself in, and I live to tell the tale. Home drive encapsulates fighting and winning the battle with depression and grief, finding not only a home you feel safe in but a body and mind you feel safe in too. I could not be prouder of tackling and overcoming the challenges arisen by my mental health, and I advocate strongly to those who are suffering to keep searching for the light in the tunnel, the rocket ship to propel you home. Keep going, you have absolutely got this, and I could not be prouder of you.

FRUIT SALAD AND ROCKET SHIPS

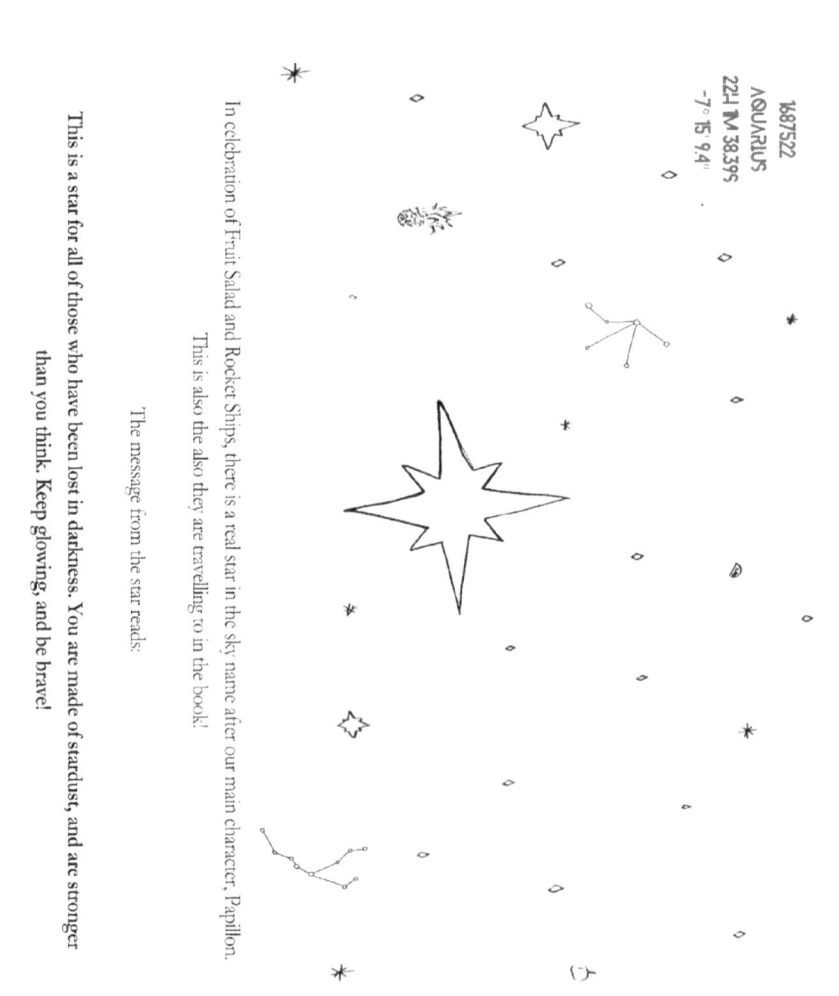

1687522
AQUARIUS
22H M 38.39S
-7° 15 9.4"

In celebration of Fruit Salad and Rocket Ships, there is a real star in the sky, name after our main character, Papillon.

This is also the they are travelling to in the book!

The message from the star reads:

This is a star for all of those who have been lost in darkness. You are made of stardust, and are stronger than you think. Keep glowing, and be brave!

Page | 111

Printed in Great Britain
by Amazon